c. Helene Smith

SUGGESTIONS FOR GROUP LEADERS

1. **THE ROOM** Discourage people from sitting behind or outside the main circle – all need to be equally involved.

2. **HOSPITALITY** Tea or coffee on arrival can be helpful at the first meeting. Perhaps at the end too, to encourage people to talk informally. Some groups might be more ambitious, taking it in turns to bring a dessert to start the evening (even in Lent, hospitality is OK!) with coffee at the end.

3. **THE START** If group members don't know each other well, some kind of 'icebreaker' might be helpful. For example, you might invite people to share something quite secular (where they grew up, holidays, hobbies, etc.). Place a time limit on this exercise.

4. **PREPARING THE GROUP** Take the group into your confidence, e.g. 'I've never done this before', or 'I've led lots of groups and each one has contained surprises'. Sharing vulnerability is designed to encourage all members to see the success of the group as their responsibility. Ask those who know that they talk easily to ration their contributions, and encourage the reticent to speak at least once or twice – however briefly. Explain that there are no 'right' answers and that among friends it is fine to say things that you are not sure about – to express half-formed ideas. However, if individuals choose to say nothing, that's all right too.

5. **THE MATERIAL** Encourage members to read each session *before* the meeting. It helps enormously if each group member has their own personal copy of this booklet (so the price is reduced either when multiple copies are ordered or if you order online). *There is no need to consider all the questions.* A lively exchange of views is what matters, so be selective. You can always spread a session over two or more meetings if you run out of time!

   For some questions you might start with a few minutes' silence to make jottings. Or you might ask members to talk in sub-groups of two or three, before sharing with the whole group.

6. **PREPARATION** Decide beforehand whether to distribute (or ask people to bring) paper, pencils, hymn books, etc. If possible, ask people in advance to read a Bible passage or lead in prayer, so that they can prepare.

7. **TIMING** Try to start on time and make sure you stick fairly closely to your stated finishing time.

8. **USING THE CD/AUDIOTAPE** There is no 'right' way! Some groups will play the 14-minute piece at the beginning of the session. Other groups do things differently – perhaps playing it at the end, or playing 7/8 minutes at the beginning and the rest halfway through the meeting. The track markers (on the CD and shown in the Transcript) will help you find any question put to the participants very easily, including the Closing Reflections, which you may wish to play (again) at the end of the session. Do whatever is best for you and your group.

SESSION 1

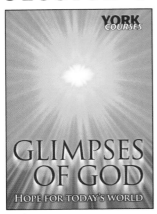

YORK COURSES

GLIMPSES OF GOD

HOPE FOR TODAY'S WORLD

THE GOD WHO HEARS OUR CRY

Early in 2010 a terrible earthquake hit the Caribbean island of Haiti. In less than a minute, most of the capital, Port au Prince, was reduced to rubble. Over 200,000 people were killed, and millions were made homeless. As the extent of the disaster became known, questions were asked. The scientists (seismologists) asked *how*: How had it happened, and how could their research help to avoid or minimise such disasters in future? The relief agencies, mobilised world-wide, asked *what*: What could they do, both immediately and in the longer term, to meet the needs of a traumatised people, feed the hungry, restore water supplies and care for the injured?

But across the world millions of ordinary people, living far away from the actual scenes of horror, simply asked *why*: Why, in a world which Christians see as created by a good and loving God, do such appalling disasters happen to innocent people? Three questions, then – *how, what* and *why*? It is the last question that hangs in the air longest.

Where is God when we need him?

Where was God when the earthquake struck Haiti? Was he unable to help? A powerless God. Or did he not care? A heartless God. Or – as many people have argued over the centuries – did he actually *cause* the earthquake in order to punish sin or simply 'teach us a lesson'? A cruel and vengeful God.

Strangely, in the event, the people of Haiti themselves didn't see things in any of those ways. One woman, rescued from beneath a wrecked house after six days entombed, could be heard to say as she was carried out on a stretcher, 'Merci, Seigneur, merci!' – 'Thank you, Lord, thank you!' On the Sunday after the disaster thousands thronged the streets of Port au Prince for open-air Masses. As one TV commentator remarked, the fragrance of the incense mingling with the stench of death. They sang 'Heaven and earth are full of your glory', but there didn't seem to be a lot of 'glory' around.

Faith seemed to flourish in that place of suffering, suggesting that the answer to the question, 'Where was God when the earthquake struck?' is: 'Right there, among the collapsing buildings'. As a vicar, I have spent time with many seriously ill and dying people, almost always conscious that God was more real and present in those circumstances than in the apparent security of daily life.

Suffering isn't pu

The idea that God
teach us a lesson
Eighteen people h
tower collapsed. 'D
who suffered in 1
others?' (Luke 13.4) ...... own question with an emphatic 'No'. Similarly, the disciples of Jesus once asked him, when faced with a man blind from birth, 'Who sinned, this man or his parents, that he was born blind?' Again, Jesus' answer was categorical: 'Neither this man nor his parents sinned' (John 9.3). So suffering is not sent by God. It isn't punishment, nor is it necessarily the result of sin – the sufferer's, or anyone else's.

Of course some suffering – quite a lot, actually – *is* the consequence of sin: war, oppression, torture, murder, cruelty, greed, exploitation ... But much suffering is simply the result of being human and living on an unpredictable planet in a purposefully 'random' universe. The unfortunate eighteen happened to be in the wrong place at the wrong time. The tower fell because ... well, sometimes towers *do* fall down. God does not 'send' disaster, nor does he normally intervene to prevent the natural course of events. They are simply part of the mysterious 'way the world is'.

But that does not mean that God is indifferent to human suffering. Far from it. The story of Moses at the Burning Bush (Exodus 3.1-4.17) makes this point very powerfully. The Israelites, of whom Moses was one, had suffered for many years as slaves in Egypt. Doubtless they'd often prayed about their plight to the God of their ancestors. Probably they wondered whether he cared about their situation; perhaps some even began to doubt his existence.

Although a Jew, Moses had been brought up in the Egyptian royal household: remember the story of the baby in the bullrushes? (Exodus 2.1-10.) But after killing an Egyptian taskmaster who was beating a Hebrew slave, Moses fled to the desert of Midian. There he met and married the daughter of a Midianite priest. Eventually, while shepherding his father-in-law's sheep, he ended up near the mountain of Sinai. He saw a bush burning – but not being consumed. Intrigued, he drew near, and was then engaged in a mysterious dialogue with God himself.

Yes, God assured him, he had heard the prayers of the Hebrew slaves. He knew about their suffering. And he was about to act to rescue them. Good news indeed. 'So come', God said, 'I will send you to Pharaoh, and bring the Israelites out of Egypt' (Exodus 3.10). God was about to act, and Moses was to be his agent. 'The cry has come to *me*, so I'm sending *you*.'

This wasn't quite how Moses had seen it! God would come down, devastate the Egyptians (a couple of decent earthquakes should do the trick) and then rescue the Israelites. Then they would be on their way to the Promised Land, which sounded quite nice really: 'a good and broad land, a land flowing with milk and honey' (Exodus 3.8). Job done.

But suddenly the rescue operation involved *him*. Moses was to confront the most powerful man in the world and persuade him to release his vast army of Hebrew slaves. God promised he would be with him, but Moses' role was crucial. God would accept no excuses – and there were plenty. The last, and most pathetic, was simply: 'O my Lord, please send someone else!' (Exodus 4.13).

Eventually Moses did agree. And after many adventures and setbacks, and some miraculous interventions by God, he led the Israelites out of Egypt, across the Red Sea and on their long journey to Canaan.

God's human agents of blessing

This story tells us a lot about the way God relates to our needs and their fulfilment. It offers answers to many of the questions we often ask: Does God know about our problems? Does he hear our prayers? Is he actually able to do anything about them? And what part does he expect us to play in answering them?

Most of us don't expect God to suspend the laws of nature and stop earthquakes, storms and floods from occurring. We do, however, expect a loving God to care about the victims of such events. The question we then face is how that care can be shown in practice. In the story of Moses at the burning bush there is no doubt about God's concern for the Hebrew slaves: 'I have heard their cry … I know their sufferings' (Exodus 3.7).

What Moses discovered was God's habitual way of meeting needs: no legions of armed angels, no well-timed earthquakes, no blinding flashes of divine light.

The problem was human. Let humans – called, supported and enabled by God – provide the answer. God would supply strength, vision and guidance. But *people* would be his agents of blessing.

Good wishes and even prayers are not enough if we – God's people – decline to be part of the practical answer to human suffering. The history of the Church is made splendid with the stories of those who have done so, from St Francis to Mother Teresa.

There are many other inspiring examples of Christians who've made a huge impact on our world. Here are a few:

- Eglantyne Jebb, who founded *Save the Children* (see box on p.8 for an example of her faith)
- Archbishop Desmond Tutu with his infectious chuckle and inspiring faith, who created the Peace and Reconciliation Commissions
- Dame Cicely Saunders, who founded the modern Hospice movement in the UK – which has now spread around the world
- Chad Varah, the London vicar who founded *Samaritans*

And there are some who may yet make a huge impact. These include:

- Rebecca Baldock, a young physiotherapist, who founded *Accomplish Children's Trust* – working with disabled children in Uganda
- Les Isaacs, a Pentecostal pastor, who founded *Street Pastors* – much praised by police and civic authorities for its work among late-night clubbers in city centres

John Young, Course editor

Earthquakes occur because tectonic plates slip from time to time. If you had a solid crust there wouldn't be any slippage; there wouldn't be any earthquakes. But there wouldn't be life for very long, because the gaps between these plates allow mineral resources to well up from within the earth and replenish its surface – keep life going. If those gaps weren't there then life would soon die out. So it's a package deal. We think it's very easy – here's the good things, keep these. Here's the bad things, throw them away. But in fact, they are mutually entangled.

Revd Professor John Polkinghorne speaking on York Courses' *CD* Hawking, Dawkins and God

QUESTIONS FOR GROUPS

BIBLE READING: Exodus 3.1-12

> *Some groups will address all the questions. That's fine. Others prefer to select just a few and spend longer on each. That's fine, too. Horses for (York) Courses!*

1. To get you started ... share with group members a time of great joy in your own life.

2. Share with group members a time of suffering in your own life and the impact it made on your faith. You might also consider what impact your faith made on your suffering.

3. **Re-read Exodus 3.10-12 and God's human agents of blessing (p. 4).** Moses' prayers resulted in a tough decision and a demanding future. On the CD [track 5; also in the Transcript] Bishop Stephen says that we shouldn't pray for anything for which we're not willing to be God's agents. Be careful what you pray for! What do you make of this in the light of your own experience?

4. On track [4] of the CD (and Transcript) Shirley Williams speaks movingly about praying for those who are ill – and the outcome of such prayers. You might discuss her experience in the light of your own.

5. **Read Romans 8.28.** Many Christians find this Bible verse sustaining in tough times. Does this verse 'speak' to you? [Tracks 7-8 on the CD find our participants grappling with this.] Are there other Bible verses which you hang on to in tough times?

6. David Wilkinson emphasises that 'faith is a living thing. It develops; it changes.' Share your own experiences of this.

7. **Read Luke 6.29 and the box at the foot of p. 3.** Where do you stand on this immense issue? [For Shirley's and Stephen's views – tracks 9 and 10.]

8. On the CD Shirley Williams describes how she combats 'compassion fatigue'. As we can't meet every plea for help, what policy do you adopt – as individuals and as a church – towards charities/Non-Governmental Organisations (NGOs) and needy individuals?

9. Hit by a falling tower? Modern society has to find someone to 'blame'. What do you make of the sharp rise in compensation claims in our 'litigious society'? In what circumstances (if any) would you sue for compensation?

10. **Read Mark 9.24 and re-read para. at foot of p.2** ('Faith seemed to flourish ...'). Suffering, bereavement and pain often bring people nearer to God, rather than driving them away. Why do you think this happens? Has anyone a personal example to share? (You may prefer to ponder this as a group in a 5-minute silence, and perhaps discuss what 'comes up'.)

11. We've probably heard people say, 'I don't know how a good God can let such things happen'. How would you respond to a friend who said this to you? See Archbishop Rowan's words in the box on p. 4.

SESSION 2

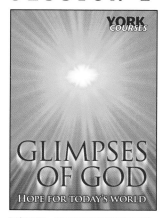

GLIMPSES
OF GOD
HOPE FOR TODAY'S WORLD

THE SHEPHERD WHO GUIDES AND GUARDS HIS PEOPLE

God does not sleep, he is never off duty, he never rests from his eternal task of guarding and guiding his people.
St Augustine of Hippo

*

The function of the shepherd is to care for the sheep, and to do and bear whatever is required for that care; the perfect shepherd faces death itself for the sheep.
Archbishop William Temple

*

The shepherd does not want safety, as long as his own people are not safe.
Archbishop Oscar Romero, Martyr

*

God isn't looking for people of great faith, but for individuals ready to follow him.
James Hudson Taylor, Victorian Missionary

Town-dwellers often have an idyllic picture of sheep and shepherds: the flock white against the green meadows; the calm shepherd guiding, protecting and feeding the sheep; the obedient dog rounding them up at his master's behest. In fact many of us have never seen an actual shepherd. They're quite rare now in that traditional rural sense, even in the British countryside.

Yet the picture remains (if only from TV) and enables people of the technological era to connect with the biblical images of God and Jesus as 'Shepherd'. 'The Lord is my shepherd,' said the psalmist (Psalm 23.1). 'I am the good shepherd,' said Jesus (John 10.11). Just as the shepherd guides and guards his flock, so the divine Shepherd leads his people and protects them from evil. It's a wonderful image, and speaks powerfully of a God who cares for us, his 'flock'.

A dangerous and demanding role

Psalm 23 is probably the best known of all the psalms. But to appreciate it fully, we need to consider the role of the shepherd in Bible times. Sheep-farming in ancient Israel was dangerous and demanding. Sheep were in constant peril – from wild animals (wolves, and even lions), hilly pathways, dangerous precipices, and even from rustlers looking for a quick return in the local meat market. Add to that the sparse nature of the grass for much of the year and the limited availability of drinking water, and we begin to understand how crucial the shepherd was. The psalm mentions help with several of these hazards (safe paths, green pastures, still waters). Jesus spoke of other perils – wolves, thieves and bandits (John 10.8-12).

So the picture of the idyllic shepherd with his tuneful pipe, sitting under a tree while the sheep munch away contentedly, turns into a scene of dedicated and demanding care. Why, said Jesus, the shepherd even 'lays down his life for the sheep' (John 10.11). The divine Shepherd cares deeply and is utterly committed to his role. If God is our shepherd, then he is a totally dedicated one.

However, you may not like thinking of yourself as a 'sheep'. Sheep are, in popular thought, docile, placid, stupid even. Incapable of making up their own minds, they simply go where they are led, eat what they are fed, and seem helpless when left to fend for themselves. That's not the kind of image we like to have of ourselves! But you have to say one thing for sheep, they're great followers. They don't argue, but simply trust their leader – and that is as good a definition of faith as you will get.

The valley of the shadow

One vivid scene in Psalm 23 makes the point very well: 'Yea, though I walk through the valley of the shadow of death, I will fear no evil: for thou art with me; thy rod and thy staff they comfort me' (AV). Stark but beautiful words. The shepherd leads the sheep out of the sunshine into the cold, dank darkness of a ravine. They're not keen to go, but they obediently follow, and eventually he leads them safely out at the other end back into the sunshine. His 'rod' pushes the reluctant ones forward; his 'staff' with its hooked end rescues any who get into trouble.

No wonder this verse has meant so much to so many down the centuries – as it did to me, when I faced the loss of my wife. There is no valley darker than that of bereavement; no shadow greater than that cast by the loss of a loved one. It's a universal experience. Few people reach middle age without experiencing this – the darkest valley we are called to walk through. It's not surprising that the very thought of it fills us with dread. Like the sheep, we prefer the sunshine.

It's interesting that neither here, nor anywhere else, does the Bible even hint that we can *avoid* that dark valley. There is no convenient bypass, no alternative route. Even the divine Shepherd can't find a way for his flock to avoid it. What he *does*, however, is promise that he will be with them in this bleak experience. 'Thou art with me.' What a reassurance! The shepherd who knows the way, who cares for his sheep, who would even die for them if necessary, does not abandon them when they are called to pass through the valley of the shadow of death. His 'rod' is there to encourage our reluctant feet; his 'staff' is there to draw us back, when in confusion or blindness we stumble off the path.

The presence of God

Of course, this whole idea of the 'presence of God' is an elusive one. How and when do we experience it? Some people talk confidently about God being 'with' them, but for many of us the idea seems rather remote from the struggles and events of daily life.

> It was only when I lay there on rotting prison straw that I sensed within myself the first stirring of good. Gradually it was disclosed to me that the line separating Good and Evil passes, not through States, not between classes, not between political parties either – but right through every human heart, and through all human hearts ... And that is why I turn back to the years of my imprisonment and say, sometimes to the astonishment of those about me: 'Bless you, prison!'
>
> *Alexander Solzhenitsyn, Nobel prize-winning author*

> The spiritual life is a gift. It is the gift of the Holy Spirit ... A spiritual life requires human effort. The forces that keep pulling us back into a worry-filled life are far from easy to overcome. A spiritual life without discipline is impossible. Discipline is the other side of discipleship. The practice of spiritual discipline makes us more sensitive to the small, gentle voice of God.
>
> *Henri J M Nouwen, Catholic Priest and Writer*

> Prayer is like watching for the Kingfisher. All you can do is be where he is likely to appear, and wait.
>
> *Ann Lewin, Poet*
>
> *
>
> You have to stalk the spirit, too. You can wait forgetful anywhere, for anywhere is the way of his fleet passage, and hope to catch him by the tail and shout something in his ear before he wrests away.
>
> *Annie Dillard, Poet and Author*

In *Some Other Rainbow*, journalist John McCarthy wrote about his years as a hostage in a dark, shuttered room in Beirut. I was surprised to read his account of an experience that I would certainly think of as the presence of God at a moment of extreme need. John describes himself as 'not conventionally religious', but in a moment of profound despair, when he felt as though he was literally falling down under its weight, he found himself crying out loud, 'God help me'. To his surprise, he was immediately aware of returning strength, of an inner renewal that was to see him through the remaining years of his captivity. For Christians, what John described was the presence of God – answering his desperate cry and standing beside him in his prison. That profound moment of 'presence' is an experience shared by many people. The divine Shepherd is never very far away and is always within earshot of our cries.

Not an 'emergency' service

For Christians, however, this can't simply be an emergency service, a sort of spiritual 999 call. It's true that you can have a phone and only use it for emergencies, but it has so many other things to offer: friendly contacts, information, messages of hope and love and reassurance from those dear to us. In our relationship with God, we can hardly build a sense of his continuing presence if we only speak to him in emergencies! As John McCarthy found, God hears our cry, and may well respond. But long-term blessing calls for long-term commitment.

Practising the presence of God

In the seventeenth century a man known as Brother Lawrence worked in the kitchen of a Carmelite priory near Paris. In that hot, tiring environment he discovered ways of cultivating a sense of God's constant presence, even when he was busy about his work. He recorded this experience in letters and conversations, which after his death were brought together in a book now considered one of the great works of Christian spirituality. It's called *The Practice of the Presence of God*, because that was how Brother Lawrence saw it. God was there, he had no doubt about that, but we need to 'practise' our awareness of him – to cultivate a sense of the divine nearness. His intensely practical approach to this is what distinguishes his spirituality from any notion of pious wishful thinking. For him, God's presence was *even more real* in the heat of the kitchen than in the quiet of the chapel.

Jesus promised that he would be with his followers always, 'to the end of the age' (Matthew 28.20). The Christian life is essentially a journey in his company. Being human, we may not always be conscious of the presence of God in our lives, but whether we are aware of it or not at any given moment, Jesus has solemnly promised it. On the last evening of his earthly life, he assured his disciples that, through the promised Holy Spirit, both his Father and he himself would be with them in the future (John 14.16-23). That promise has never been withdrawn.

As World Affairs Editor at the BBC John Simpson has been in the thick of many wars. On TV on Armistice Day 2010 John commented, 'I've found that my faith as an Anglican has been profoundly helpful'. In 2003 he narrowly escaped death when he and his television crew were hit by 'friendly fire' in Iraq. Fifteen people were killed – including Kamaran Abdurazaq Muhamed, the local translator he'd hired. Despite years of experience, John was extremely distressed and suffered 'survivor guilt'. He knew that if he hadn't hired Kamaran, the interpreter would still be alive. As the months passed he felt the need to find some peace about it all. In the end, this peace came from his faith: '*It was just sitting in church and talking to my vicar about it that eventually made me come to terms with what was happening. And the vicar in particular was very anxious to say – I remember the gesture – "God holds Kamaran to him as much now as before"*.'

From *Lord … Help My Unbelief* by John Young

When I think of London, I visualise Big Ben. Because London is so vast I have to cut it down to size. So it is with 'God talk'. The key to understanding the way verbal images 'work' in the Bible is to take one central point. When we call God 'Shepherd', we are focusing on his love and care – not on the woolliness of the sheep! When we call God a 'rock' we're not suggesting that God is inanimate, but that he is strong and dependable. The Psalms and John's Gospel are full of verbal images for God and for Jesus. You might care to draw up a list and reflect upon their significance. This makes a very interesting Bible study.

John Young, Course editor

QUESTIONS FOR GROUPS
BIBLE READING: Psalm 23

1. 'Just as the shepherd guides, guards and feeds his flock, so the divine Shepherd leads his people.' As you look back over your life, can you discern the guiding hand of God? How does God guide, in your experience? (You might like to replay David Wilkinson's take on this [track 16]).

2. **Re-read Romans 8.28 and the Solzhenitzyn box on p.9**. In the light of these, what do you make of the bad things that have happened in your life?

3. 'They [sheep] don't argue but simply trust their leader – and that is as good a definition of faith as you will get.' Can you give an example of faith in action from your own life – or the life of someone else?

4. **Re-read Psalm 23.4**. 'This verse has meant so much to so many down the centuries – as it did to me, when I faced the loss of my wife.' Group members are invited to share experiences of faith and bereavement – their own or other people's.

5. **Read Matthew 28.20**. What other dark valleys are there (e.g. redundancy)? Group members might like to share times of testing – and discuss the significance of faith and/or doubt at such times.

6. 'Some people talk confidently about God being "with" them, but for many of us the idea seems rather remote from the struggles and events of daily life.' Lucy Winkett talks of the 'God who is our friend …' [track 25]. Bishop Stephen says, 'I do believe Jesus is with me always. But it doesn't always *feel* like that.' Can you identify with any of these statements?

7. 'There aren't many atheists in a lifeboat'! How do group members feel about '999' emergency prayers? Again, any personal experiences?

8. Re-read and discuss the paragraph 'not an "emergency" service' and the quote from Henri Nouwen (both on p.9). If you were asked by a younger Christian for help with regular prayer, how would you reply?

9. What do you make of John McCarthy's answered prayer (p.9)? Many Christians do not have dramatic spiritual experiences, although some do. You're invited to share your own experience of God – dramatic or otherwise.

10. **Read John 10.11.** Bible passages like this and Psalm 23 used to inform the nation's consciousness. Is Britain still – as David Cameron asserts – a Christian country? (You might wish to listen again to tracks 22-24, either before or after you've discussed this question.)

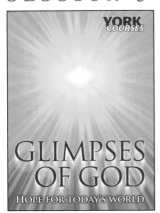

YORK COURSES

GLIMPSES OF GOD

HOPE FOR TODAY'S WORLD

THE SON WHO IS THE WAY, THE TRUTH AND THE LIFE

[The Nun's] constant phrase, 'Go with God', had puzzled me. Suddenly it became clear. It was a revelation – acceptance. It filled me with joy. Accept life, the world, Spirit, God, call it what you will, and all else will follow ... Those three small words, 'Go with God', were for me the beginning of faith. That evening I started to read the Gospels.

Jennifer Worth (in Call the Midwife, *also a TV series)*

The God who hears our cries; the God who guides our path ... Now we think about the God who makes himself known to us. That in itself is an amazing concept: that the Creator of the Universe, the infinite power that brought all things into being, actually *wants* us to know what he's like and invites us to come to him.

This is the great invitation of the Bible. 'If you seek me with all your heart, you will find me' (Jeremiah 29.13). 'Ask and it will be given to you, seek and you will find, knock and it will be opened to you' (Matthew 7.7). It is up to us human beings to do the seeking, asking, and knocking. But it is up to Almighty God to show himself to us and invite us to come into his presence.

More dramatically, sometimes the invitation is put the other way round. 'Listen, I am standing at the door knocking,' says Jesus in one of Revelation's less complicated visions (3.20). He's outside the lukewarm church at Laodicea. 'If you hear my voice', he says, 'and open the door, I will come in to you and eat with you, and you with me.' Holman Hunt painted the scene, and it's often used by evangelists to urge people to 'ask Jesus into their lives'. Fair enough. But in fact it's a whole Church that's inside, and the Son of God who's outside. And – this is the point – he's pleading to be let in.

So the God of the Bible is a God who *wants* to be known. He's not a 'secret' God, but a God of revelation. Obviously we can't 'understand' him. We can't work him out or discover him with our microscopes and telescopes. If God is almighty and all-knowing (and what sort of 'god' would he be if he weren't?) we are dependent on him to let us know what he is like. The universal witness of the Bible is that he has done that – though gradually, and over long ages.

From glimpses to the full picture

In other words, God's revelation to us has been progressive. That is to say, our picture of God has got clearer as time has passed and people have experienced his ways. For long ages our understanding of God was fragmentary and partial, but the Bible takes us from glimpses of the truth to a clearer vision and finally to the full picture: 'God, who gave to our forefathers many different glimpses of the truth, has now, at the end of the present age, given us the truth in

YORK COURSES
ECUMENICAL COURSES FOR ENQUIRING MINDS

... bringing leading Christian thinkers into your discussion groups

GLIMPSES OF GOD
Hope for today's world

Course booklet written by Canon David Winter

We live in turbulent times. This course draws on the Bible, showing where we can find strength and encouragement as we live through the 21st century.

FIVE SESSIONS: The God who hears our cry; The Shepherd who guides and guards his people; The Son who is the Way, Truth and Life; The God who shares our pain; The God who calms our fears

With Rt Hon Shirley Williams, Bishop Stephen Cottrell, Revd Professor David Wilkinson. Closing Reflections by Revd Lucy Winkett. Introduced by Dr David Hope.

HANDING ON THE TORCH
Sacred words for a secular world

Course booklet written by Canon John Young

FIVE SESSIONS: A Christian Country? A Secular Society? A Beleaguered Church? Competing Creeds? Handing on the Torch

Christianity continues to grow at an immense pace – especially in Asia (including China), Africa and Latin America. At the same time in the West it struggles to grow and – perhaps – even to survive. We consider some of the reasons and what it might mean for individual Christians, churches and Western culture, in a world where alternative beliefs are increasingly on offer.

With Archbishop Sentamu, Clifford Longley, Rachel Lampard. Introduced by Dr David Hope. Closing Reflections by Bishop Graham Cray

RICH INHERITANCE
Jesus' legacy of love

Course booklet written by Bishop Stephen Cottrell

FIVE SESSIONS: An empty tomb; A group of people; A story; A power; A meal

Jesus left no written instructions. He didn't seem to have a plan. At the end, as he hung dying on the cross, almost all of his followers had abandoned him. By most worldly estimates his ministry was a failure. Nevertheless, Jesus' message of reconciliation with God lives on. With this good news his disciples changed the world. How did they do it? What else did Jesus leave behind – what is his 'legacy of love'?

with Archbishop Vincent Nichols, Paula Gooder, Jim Wallis. Introduced by Dr David Hope. Closing Reflections by Inderjit Bhogal

OUR EASY-TO-USE COURSES FOR GROUP DISCU

WHEN I SURVEY...
Christ's cross and ours

FIVE SESSIONS: Darkness at Noon; Into Great Silence; The Child on the Cross; Outside a City Wall; Touching the Rock

The death of Christ is a dominant and dramatic theme in the New Testament. The death of Jesus is not the end of a track – it's the gateway into life.

with **General Sir Richard Dannatt, John Bell, Christina Baxter.** *Introduced by* **Dr David Hope.** *Closing Reflections by* **Colin Morris.** *Course booklet written by the* **Revd Dr John Pridmore**

These three... FAITH, HOPE & LOVE

FIVE SESSIONS: Believing and trusting; The Peace of God; Faith into Love; The Greatest of these; All shall be well

Based on the three great qualities celebrated in 1 Corinthians 13.

with **Bishop Tom Wright, Anne Atkins, The Abbot of Worth.** *Closing Reflections by* **Professor Frances Young.** *Introduced by* **Dr David Hope**

THE LORD'S PRAYER
praying it, meaning it, living it

FIVE SESSIONS: Our Father; Thy will be done; Our daily bread; As we forgive; In heaven

In the Lord's Prayer Jesus gives us a pattern for living as his disciples. It also raises vital questions for today's world in which 'daily bread' is uncertain for billions and a refusal to 'forgive those who trespass against us' escalates violence.

with **Canon Margaret Sentamu, Bishop Kenneth Stevenson, Dr David Wilkinson.** *Closing Reflections by* **Dr Elaine Storkey.** *Introduced by* **Dr David Hope**

CAN WE BUILD A BETTER WORLD?

FIVE SESSIONS: Slavery – then and now; Friendship & Prayer – then and now; Change & Struggle – then and now; The Bible – then and now; Redemption & Restitution – then and now

We live in a divided world and with a burning question. As modern Christians can we – together with others of good will – build a better world? Important material for important issues.

with **Archbishop John Sentamu, Wendy Craig, Leslie Griffiths. Five Poor Clares from BBC TV's The Convent.** *Introduced by* **Dr David Hope**

WHERE IS GOD...?

FIVE SESSIONS: Where is God when we ... seek happiness? ... face suffering? ... make decisions? ... contemplate death? ... try to make sense of life?

To find honest answers to these big questions we need to undertake some serious and open thinking. Where better to do this than with trusted friends in a study group around this course?

with **Archbishop Rowan Williams, Patricia Routledge** CBE, **Joel Edwards, Dr Pauline Webb.** *Introduced by* **Dr David Hope**

BETTER TOGETHER?

FIVE SESSIONS: Family Relationships; Church Relationships; Relating to Strangers; Broken Relationships; Our Relationship with God

All about relationships – in the church and within family and society. *Better Together?* looks at how the Christian perspective may differ from that of society at large.

with **the Abbot of Ampleforth, John Bell, Nicky Gumbel, Jane Williams.** *Introduced by* **Dr David Hope**

TOUGH TALK Hard Sayings of Jesus

FIVE SESSIONS: Shrinking and Growing; Giving and Using; Praying and Forgiving; Loving and Telling; Trusting and Entering

Looks at many of the hard sayings of Jesus in the Bible and faces them squarely. His uncomfortable words need to be faced if we are to allow the full impact of the gospel on our lives.

with **Bishop Tom Wright, Steve Chalke, Fr Gerard Hughes SJ, Professor Frances Young.** *Introduced by* **Dr David Hope**

NEW WORLD, OLD FAITH

FIVE SESSIONS: Brave New World?;
Environment and Ethics; Church and Family in Crisis?;
One World – Many Faiths;
Spirituality and Superstition

How does Christian faith continue to shed light on a range of issues in our changing world, including change itself? This course helps us make sense of our faith in God in today's world.

*with **Archbishop Rowan Williams, David Coffey, Joel Edwards, Revd Dr John Polkinghorne** KBE FRS, **Dr Pauline Webb.** Introduced by **Dr David Hope***

IN THE WILDERNESS

FIVE SESSIONS: Jesus, Satan and the Angels;
The Wilderness Today; The Church in the Wilderness; Prayer, Meditation and Scripture;
Solitude, Friendship and Fellowship

Like Jesus, we all have wilderness experiences. What are we to make of these challenges? *In the Wilderness* explores these issues for our world, for the church, and at a personal level.

*with **Cardinal Cormac Murphy-O'Connor, Archbishop David Hope, Revd Dr Rob Frost, Roy Jenkins, Dr Elaine Storkey***

FAITH IN THE FIRE

FIVE SESSIONS: Faith facing Facts;
Faith facing Doubt; Faith facing Disaster;
Faith fuelling Prayer; Faith fuelling Action

When things are going well our faith may remain untroubled, but what if doubt or disaster strike? Those who struggle with faith will find they are not alone.

*with **Archbishop David Hope, Rabbi Lionel Blue, Steve Chalke, Revd Dr Leslie Griffiths, Ann Widdecombe** MP*

JESUS REDISCOVERED

FIVE SESSIONS: Jesus' Life and Teaching;
Following Jesus; Jesus: Saviour of the World;
Jesus is Lord; Jesus and the Church

Re-discovering who Jesus was, what he taught, and what that means for his followers today. Some believers share what Jesus means to them.

*with **Paul Boateng** MP, **Dr Lavinia Byrne, Joel Edwards, Bishop Tom Wright, Archbishop David Hope***

LIVE YOUR FAITH

SIX SESSIONS: The Key - Jesus; Prayer;
The Community - the Church;
The Dynamic - the Holy Spirit; The Bible;
The Outcome - Service & Witness

Christianity isn't just about what we believe: it's about how we live. A course suitable for everyone; particularly good for enquirers and those in the early stages of their faith.

*with **Revd Dr Donald English, Lord Tonypandy, Fiona & Roy Castle***

GREAT EVENTS, DEEP MEANINGS

SIX SESSIONS: Christmas; Ash Wednesday; Palm Sunday; Good Friday; Easter; Pentecost

Explains clearly what the feasts and fasts are about and challenges us to respond spiritually and practically. There are even a couple of quizzes to get stuck into!

*with **Revd Dr John Polkinghorne** KBE FRS, **Gordon Wilson, Bishop David Konstant, Fiona Castle, Dame Cicely Saunders, Archbishop David Hope***

PRICES FOR OUR COURSES

Held till 1st June 2013. Free 2nd class P&P in UK OR add £2 for 1st class P&P.

BOOKLET:	**£3.90**	*(**£3.40** each for **5** or more)*
CD:	**£10.99**	*(**£8.99** each for **2** or more)*
AUDIOTAPE:	**£8.99**	*(**£6.99** each for **5** or more)*
TRANSCRIPT:	**£4.99**	*(**£3.10** each for **2** or more)*

CD TASTER PACK: £17.65 – **save £2.23**

Each group needs 1 CD or audiotape, plus a course booklet for each member. In addition many groups find the transcript booklet extremely helpful.

his Son' (Hebrews 1.1-2). That, in a nutshell, is the story of the Bible – from glimpses to the whole picture.

But how exactly are we supposed to 'see' God or 'find' him? The human search for God, as the Bible relates it, has followed many paths. One is the lived experience of those who believe in him and live by that belief. Somehow, we can often 'see God' in them. For other people the path is the mystery of our very existence.

Looking at Creation

When we look with senses alert at Creation, we may share the awe and wonder of the Psalmist: 'The heavens are telling the glory of God; and the firmament proclaims his handiwork' (Psalm 19.1). In the New Testament the letter to the Romans makes the same point even more directly: 'Ever since the creation of the world his eternal power and divine nature, invisible though they are, have been understood and seen through the things he has made' (Romans 1.20). Until modern times this was for most people a convincing argument for a Creator.

However, in today's scientific and technological world, people tend to be more sceptical about this as evidence for a 'personal' God, even while marvelling at the vast infinity of space and the amazing order and beauty of the natural world. It is, after all, one thing to believe that God exists. It is quite another to believe that we can 'know' him, or that he makes himself known to us. Christians don't believe in a kind of cosmic dynamo or supernatural mastermind, but in a personal God who actually knows and loves his creatures.

The Scriptures

So most of us need a more specific path to the knowledge of God, and that is offered in the Bible. In these writings we have, as it were, an inspired scrapbook of the human race's experience of God. Here are records, stories, visions, poems and songs which tell how, down the ages, people have encountered the Divine. Some of it will be more relevant to us today than other parts, but it would be a cold heart that isn't stirred by this record of humankind's long search for the ultimate prize: the unfolding revelation of the nature of our Creator.

From search to discovery

For most of us, turning that search into discovery is the real problem. It seems that the first disciples of Jesus also found this problematic. When Jesus told them that they already 'knew' the way to the Father in heaven, Thomas said, 'Lord, we don't know where you are going. How can we know the way?' Jesus replied in memorable words, 'I am the way, and the truth, and the life' (John 14.5-6).

'I am the way' is a strange expression. Jesus didn't say 'I'll show you the way', or 'I'll point you in the right direction'. That's what great prophets and religious teachers of the past had done. Jesus simply said, 'I am the way.' So what did he mean?

Years ago I worked in Jerusalem for a couple of weeks. A colleague asked an Arab man in the street the way to the Damascus Gate. The man didn't point or give directions. He took him by the elbow and said, 'I am the way'. He *led him there*! Jesus is the way in the sense that he is the path and – more than that – the guide-companion. He 'takes us to God'.

So the culmination of our search for God is his Son, Jesus. In fact, he made this astonishing claim to his disciples: 'Whoever has seen me has seen the Father' (John 14.9). It is a staggering claim, but it has stood the test of time. If you want to know what God is like, look at Jesus.

So those very Scriptures which, as we have seen, in their varied ways point to the God we seek, finally tell us the story of Jesus. The New Testament writers pass on to us today the impact and meaning of his amazing life on those who knew him and followed him on earth. Jesus is, they would claim, the culmination of the human search for God, and of God's search for us.

What are you seeking?

Early in John's Gospel there's a scene with all the hallmarks of authentic personal memory. Two followers of John the Baptist heard him say, as Jesus walked by, 'Look, here's the Lamb of God!' (John 1.35-36). So they followed this person to find out more. As they trailed Jesus, he turned and asked them what they were seeking. 'Rabbi [Teacher], where are you staying?' was their rather inept reply. Possibly they meant, 'Can we come and spend some time with you?' Anyway, Jesus' answer was clear and inviting: 'Come and see.'

Holman Hunt's famous picture *The Light of the World* illustrates Revelation 3.20. The doorway is overgrown and there is no handle on the outside, suggesting that Jesus can enter our lives only if we open the door and invite him in …

We are grateful to the Chapter of St Paul's Cathedral for allowing us to reproduce the painting below.

Come and see!

In a sense, that's always been the divine invitation. You're looking for answers, explanations. Your 'god' is a mystery, sometimes a frightening one. If there is a Creator, a heavenly Power who shapes our lives, what is he (or she or it) like? Well, 'Come and see!' Look at the world you live in. Lift your eyes to the stars. Look into your own imagination, and that of others. See the signs of love in human relationships, the touch of a friendly hand, the enfolding arms of a nursing mother. Best of all – as those disciples were to discover – Jesus says, look at *me*. When you do, you may begin to see God. Come and see!

QUESTIONS FOR GROUPS

BIBLE READING: John 14.1-10

1. On track [26] of the CD/Transcript Shirley Williams describes a rather dramatic answer to prayer. Have you experienced anything like that?

2. Faith is often described as a journey. Share where you think you are on that journey: just starting out, on the way, nearly there, struggling, arrived … What are the hindrances on the road? And what have you found to be helpful?

3. **Read Luke 15.11-32.** What do we learn about God from this famous parable? You might care to discuss one or two other Bible passages which have helped you to understand God better.

4. **Read Matthew 10.42 and 25.36.** Mother Teresa saw God in the faces of the poor. On the CD Stephen Cottrell says he tries to see Christ in everyone he meets. Some people find this very difficult! What about people we don't like? What about violent people?

5. Was/is the Church a help or a hindrance in your search for God, and in your own journey into faith? Do you believe that God searches for us – perhaps before we search for him? (See *Hound of Heaven* poem extract in box below.)

6. **Read 1 Corinthians 15.22.** Does John 14.6 exclude non-Christians from God's presence? You might find it helpful to listen again to track [27] where that question is discussed and read the boxes on p. 14.

7. **Read James 2.19.** 'Believing' in God has two quite separate meanings: believing that he exists; and putting our faith in him. Can you tease out the distinction? What practical difference might either of these make to our lives?

8. In which other ways, places or circumstances, have members of the group experienced 'glimpses of God'? Nature, love, worship, music …? Specific examples, please!

9. **Read Revelation 3.14-20.** Read the Holman Hunt box on p.15. How does this relate to your experience of faith and life?

10. **Read John 1.39.** 'Come and see!' The annual 'Back to Church Sunday' builds on this. How do you feel about using this opportunity? Draw up a list of folk you might consider inviting. Do you think your church is ready for this? Might other Sundays be better? E.g. Mothering Sunday, Harvest Festival, Carol Service …

11. Listen again to tracks [30-32] and discuss leadership. What is (or should be) our part in supporting and encouraging leaders?

I fled Him down the nights and down the days
I fled Him down the arches of the years
I fled Him down the labyrinthine ways
Of my own mind, and in the midst of tears
I hid from him, and under running laughter…

Francis Thompson (opening lines of *The Hound of Heaven*)

SESSION 4

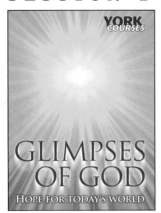

THE GOD WHO SHARES OUR PAIN

In this course we've been reflecting on the God who hears our cry; the God who cares for his people; the God who invites us to come to him. Now we consider one of the most poignant and revealing scenes in the whole of the Bible. Jesus' betrayal in the Garden of Gethsemane (Mark 14.43-46) reveals the most amazing truth of all: our God not only understands our pain and suffering – but actually *shares* it.

We all know that life inevitably includes the experience of injustice, pain, sorrow and sickness. How can the God who is Creator of the Universe understand what it is like to be human, to be weak and vulnerable, to be let down by friends, to feel frightened and misunderstood, to be wracked with pain, or to face death?

That question was answered in two places: Gethsemane (where Jesus wept and prayed before his betrayal by Judas) and Calvary (where he was crucified). In that quiet garden, and on that ugly hill, we discover that our Creator not only understands our cries for help, not only guides and cares for us through the dark valleys of life, *but has himself experienced the pain, the injustice, the weakness and vulnerability* that are so evidently a part of human existence. Only through what we call the 'incarnation' – the presence of God in a human life in the person of his Son Jesus – could that possibly be true. It is in the events of that fateful night and the following day that the ultimate mystery of the love of God is fully revealed in the suffering and death of his Son.

The garden of tears

After the 'last supper' which the disciples shared with Jesus, he led them across the city, through the Temple courts and up the Mount of Olives to a garden they had often used as a place of prayer. Gethsemane, an ancient garden with olive trees, is still there: it remains a popular site for Christian pilgrims. Jesus took three of the disciples, Peter, James and John, deeper into the garden with him, having instructed the others to sit and pray. He told the three that he was 'deeply grieved, even to death' and asked them to remain at that spot and keep awake, while he went off to pray on his own. Then, a short distance from them, he 'threw himself on the ground', wept bitterly, and prayed a simple but painful prayer. '*Abba*, Father, for you all things are possible; remove this cup from me; yet, not what I want, but what you want' (Mark 14.36).

During his state visit to Britain in September 2010 Pope Benedict said:

'My predecessor, the late Pope John Paul, suffered very publicly during the last years of his life. It was clear to all of us that he did so in union with the sufferings of our Saviour. His cheerfulness and forbearance as he faced his final days were a remarkable and moving example to all of us who have to carry the burden of advancing years.'

The 'cup' of which he spoke is the 'cup' of Psalm 75.8 – the cup of God's indignation at the presence of sin in his world. That cup is bitter, and Jesus knew that it was his task, as the Suffering Servant prophesied by Isaiah, to drink it. (He had already spoken of this to two of these disciples: see Mark 10.38-39.) Jesus had repeatedly warned the Twelve that he was destined to die in Jerusalem, but now the moment was imminent Jesus was profoundly troubled at the appalling prospect. This prayer is drawn from a troubled heart. It is the clearest example in the Gospels of the inner battle which the Son of God had to face, as well as the external cost of physical pain and humiliation. Was there not, he was asking, some other way? Did it *have* to be the cross?

Yet he instantly added the words that we find hardest to add, particularly in times of desperate need: 'Yet, not what I want, but what you want.' He knew he was not addressing a remote, grim God who was looking to punish him or cause him pain, but the one he called '*Abba*, Father'. He knew he was loved, within the unity of the Trinity, as we can know that we are loved within the unity of God's family. He also knew that the only safe place, the only place of real security, is in the will of his Father.

Jesus prayed, while his disciples – sadly – dozed off. So the great inner battle of trust was faced and won alone. He rose from the ground strengthened, ready to face Judas and the temple guard, and all the dark consequences on the following day. The offering was finally made on Calvary (the hill of the skull) but it seems that the real battle had been won the previous evening – in the Garden of Gethsemane.

'For God so loved the world...'

My Song is Love Unknown is one of my favourite hymns, but I simply can't accept one line in it: 'Joyful he to suffering goes'. There's nothing 'joyful' about that desperate prayer in Gethsemane. In that moment the Son of God knelt and shared exactly the same burden of fear, anxiety, pain and longing that we feel *in extremis*. Someone dear to us is ill or dying. We have just been given some terrible news – an accident, perhaps, or even a suicide. We are in turmoil. 'Oh God, *why?*' we cry to the heavens. We know we should add those words of Jesus, but we just can't: 'yet, not my will but yours'. It is when we are in that situation that the Jesus of Gethsemane becomes so precious. God knows how we're feeling, because in his beloved Son he's been there before us.

Stuart Hallam, himself a trained Commando, when a chaplain in Afghanistan, said: 'Being a Christian is about sharing in God's incarnation, even in the darkest of dark places – keeping the rumour of God alive, despite what life might seem to be telling us.' He bases his ministry on the great First World War Chaplain, Woodbine Willie, who said, 'Live with the men, go where they go ... share in their risks... The best place for a padre is where there is the most danger of death.'

'...vulnerable, elderly people may feel they have become a burden and, once legal prohibitions are removed, under pressure to end their lives. It is significant that organisations that serve the elderly and disabled remain strongly opposed to changing the law on assisted dying.

Dr Elaine Storkey

In *God of the Valley* Steve Griffiths wrote about Graham Sutherland's tapestry of *Christ in Glory* in Coventry Cathedral: 'Half of the face is beautiful and glorified; half of the face is charred and burnt. That ... is a perfect representation of glory – a mixture of beauty and pain. The risen Christ ascended to heaven and was glorified at the right hand of God. But even now, he wears the marks of crucifixion and the scarred persona of one who has borne our pain so that we might know forgiveness, healing and reconciliation.'

Jesus had constantly warned his disciples about what lay ahead for him: '… the Son of Man will be handed over to the chief priests and the scribes, and they will condemn him to death; then they will hand him over to the Gentiles; they will mock him, and spit upon him, and flog him, and kill him; and after three days he will rise again' (Mark 10.33-34).

It was only now, as they sensed the sombre mood of Jesus, that they seemed fully to understand what he was saying. But beyond doubt, Jesus knew. And yet, faced with betrayal, rank injustice, abuse and then the most appalling and cruel death, he could pray, 'Not my will, but yours be done' (Luke 22.42). The clue to that faith is surely in that one word '*Abba*'. The prayer of Jesus was not addressed to a cosmic source of power, the Lord of Hosts or the King of Glory (though God is all of those) but to '*Abba*', the homely, intimate Aramaic word for 'father'. It is the word a child would use, climbing on to a father's lap.

Infinite agony; infinite love

It was to the God of infinite love that Jesus addressed his prayer of infinite agony, in the utter certainty that whatever the response to that prayer might be, it would be motivated by the supremacy of love. It was for love that Jesus was to die – love of God's fallen creatures. It was for love of us that God gave his Son: 'God so loved the world that he gave …' (John 3.16). And it was in the hands of that love that Jesus would walk the *via dolorosa* (the path of sorrows) and go to the hill of the skull to die.

There is, of course, a profound truth about God and human need in the events of that evening and the following day. Just about every aspect of human sorrow was experienced by Jesus. He was betrayed by his close companion, deserted by his male friends (who all 'forsook him and fled'), unjustly condemned for crimes of which he was innocent, abused and flogged by men who knew nothing about him, and led out to public humiliation and execution.

It's very natural for us, in a situation of despair, to say to God, 'You can't know what it's like.' He can. He's been there. The incarnate Son has known what it is to suffer. And, at the heart of that experience of suffering, he has also known what it is to put himself into the hands of his heavenly Father. 'Not my will, but yours' is probably the most difficult prayer of all to pray. But for us, as for Jesus, it can be the prayer that unlocks the floodgates of faith.

19

QUESTIONS FOR GROUPS

BIBLE READING: Hebrews 4.14-16 and 12.1-3

1. Shirley Williams talks of prayerful meditation during tough times, and of being an 'unmethodical pray-er' – as well as falling asleep! Can you relate to any or all of these?

2. **Re-read Hebrews 12.2-3.** Most of us have experienced suffering – whether physical or emotional. Did the knowledge that the Son of God has also suffered bring comfort to you at those times? If so, how?

3. **Read John 10.11-15.** The Good Shepherd lays down his life for the sheep. Reflect upon Good Friday and the way you like to spend it. Share the importance of the death of Jesus to you personally.

4. **Read Mark 14.35-36.** The prayer of Jesus in Gethsemane is unlike any other image of divinity – the horror of death, the desperate prayer for a way of escape, and the courageous acceptance that his Father's will is best. What does this tell us about God? And what does it tell us about suffering?

5. **Read Psalm 10.1 and Psalm 13.** We talk to God; how do we know God is listening? Some psalms are more turbulent than Psalm 23: they express bewilderment, even anger, as well as hope and faith. How honest do you feel you can be with God in prayer – telling him just 'how it is' for you?

6. Gethsemane. A place of decision – and of indecision. A place of courage – and of fear. Have you had a Gethsemane moment, when you faced a huge decision – or faced your own personal demons? How did your faith 'work' on that occasion?

7. **Read Luke 22.41-44** and listen to track [39] on the CD. Does the fact that Jesus wanted to avoid the suffering ahead offer you any comfort?

8. Suffering sometimes drives people away from God. But quite often it turns people towards God. Why do you think this is? And can you illustrate from people you've met?

9. The cross and grave are not the end of the story. The Jesus of Gethsemane is also the Jesus of the empty tomb and the Resurrection. Discuss the elements you want in your own funeral. How might you emphasise your Christian belief in heaven?

10. Jesus prayed alone, and went to the hill called Calvary alone. Have you ever experienced deep loneliness? As individuals, or as a group or church, how might you identify and help those who are lonely?

11. **Read Luke 22.54-62.** The New Testament is remarkably frank in recording that the disciples failed Jesus. Does their weakness depress or reassure you – or a bit of both?

12. Shirley Williams says that 'suicide is always wrong', while David Wilkinson says 'I wouldn't want to say it's a sin'. What do you think? This might be too painful for some groups, who may prefer to discuss assisted dying – so much in the news. Where do you stand on this? How does your Christian faith inform your judgement?

> Suicide is much more common than we seem to imagine. World-wide, one million people kill themselves every year. The World Health Organisation says that it is the thirteenth most common cause of death. It is the leading cause of death among men under the age of 35 in the UK.
>
> *Paul Vallely, Journalist*

SESSION 5

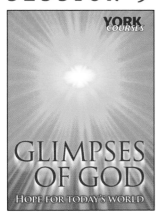

GLIMPSES OF GOD
HOPE FOR TODAY'S WORLD

THE GOD WHO CALMS OUR FEARS

In a 2005 USA Gallup poll, 13-15 year olds were asked to list their top ten fears. You might like to draw up a list of possibilities before turning to their answers on p. 23.

One evening a mother asked her little boy to bring a broom in from the garage. He responded, "I don't want to go out there. It's getting dark!" She smiled reassuringly. "You don't have to be afraid of the dark," she explained. "Jesus is out there. He'll look after you and protect you." The little boy thought about that and opened the back door a fraction. Peering into the darkness he called, "Jesus? If you're out there, would you please hand me the broom?"

One of Andrew Lloyd-Webber's musicals is called *Aspects of Love*, and I did for a time consider 'stealing' that name for this course. 'God is love,' the Bible says, so every aspect of God is an aspect of Love. We have considered the God who hears our cry, the God who guides and guards, the God who makes himself known and the God who shares our pain. All of these are 'aspects of love': what we would like to do for those we love, if we could. This last session looks at yet another aspect of love: the love that calms our fears.

'Don't worry, don't be afraid,' sometimes seems the most pointless piece of advice we can receive. When the consultant says, 'I don't want to worry you' the next word is always 'but': 'but I'd like to run some more tests', or, 'but I'd like you to see the oncologist'. Usually, when someone tells us not to worry it's because we *are* worried, and often with reason. Without action to substantiate the words, the mere advice is empty comfort.

Everyday worries

At a recent Bible study on Matthew 6, in which Jesus lists all the things we shouldn't be anxious about, one group member pointed out that those were exactly the things people *do* worry about – and often with good reason. Food? What if there's nothing in the larder and no money to buy some? Clothes? Supposing you're not able to afford a winter coat and the weather is freezing? Health? What about that chilling moment when you realise that you, or someone you love, is desperately – even terminally – ill?

The final example cited by Jesus was 'tomorrow': why worry about tomorrow? But, in our scary, chancy world, what is more natural than to be anxious about what has not happened yet, but well might?

So was Jesus unrealistic, or at any rate over-optimistic, about the degree of faith humans can be expected to summon up? And was 'summoning up enough faith' what Jesus was talking about? As someone has said, a little faith in a big God is better than a lot of faith in a little one. Jesus himself said that faith as small as a grain of mustard seed is enough if it is true faith in God. In the light of that, what does it mean when we claim that trusting God calms our fears?

Jesus constantly told his disciples, 'Fear not', or 'Don't worry'. He said it to them in many different circumstances. They were not to worry when their boat was sinking; not

> When I look back on all these worries, I remember the story of the old man who said on his deathbed that he had had a lot of troubles in his life, most of which never happened.
>
> *Sir Winston Churchill*
>
> *
>
> God says: Give me your worries. I've got everything else. *Rabbi Lionel Blue*
>
> *
>
> Grief has limits, whereas apprehension has none. For we grieve only for what we know has happened, but we fear all that possibly may happen.
>
> *Pliny the Younger (born 61 AD)*

> You can become more fearful [of terrorism] and protective of your lifestyle and your loved ones, or you come to terms with the fact that open and tolerant societies will always come with their own risks. These societies flourish because we put our trust in people, in authorities and in places.
>
> *Prof. Mona Siddiqui*

> My faith is a really important part of my life and has been a real backbone through lots of difficult times… For me as a teenager to know this song [*Amazing Grace*] and to realise that faith doesn't have to be soppy and wet and actually there could be strength in it was very powerful… I've been so grateful for that quiet presence of great friends and also my Christian faith.
>
> *Bear Grylls, TV Adventurer*

to worry at the prospect of their Master and Lord leaving them; not to worry when they saw Jesus walking on the water; not to worry at the vision of Jesus transfigured in glory, or at various miraculous events, or at the awesome sight of the risen Lord in the upper room. Every one of those situations would almost certainly create anxiety or outright fear in any normal human being. Yet Jesus said, 'Fear not … Don't be afraid.'

Empty comfort?

And this was not empty comfort. When Jesus was with them and they heard his words, they were no longer afraid. When a child wakes from a nasty dream and cries out in the darkness, the arrival of mum or dad has an instantly calming effect. The one who knows and loves them has heard. But it's more than that. The one now sitting on the bed, or giving the child a cuddle, represents security, strength and experience. The dream simply fades away in the light of a familiar and loving presence, someone who knows them – and knows all about nasty dreams!

When Jesus walked across the waves to his disciples in their storm-battered little boat, his first words were not to still the storm on the lake, but the storm in their hearts. 'Why are you afraid?' The interior storm was calmed by his presence; then the storm on the waters was calmed by his words of power.

Fear paralyses. 'Don't worry' seems a puny message in the face of our fears, real and actual – or imaginary. Yet there it is on the lips of Jesus, time and again. And because he was the one who spoke it, because his hearers trusted his security, strength and experience and knew that he loved them, they were reassured. Like the child in the night, they found their fears and anxieties banished. He knew what he was talking about, and they trusted him.

That is not to say that the fears were not real. There *was* a storm on the lake and the boat *was* in danger of sinking. The sudden appearance of a man whom they had seen executed 48 hours earlier *was* frightening, by any estimation. When John, the author of Revelation, had a vision of the risen Christ he tells us that he 'fell at his feet as though dead' (Revelation 1.17).

Facing our fears

We don't conquer our fears by pretending they don't exist. Unless I've completely misunderstood it, that is the heart of the message of that strange book of Revelation. The 'four horsemen of the apocalypse' still ride through the lands, bringing injustice, war, plague and violent death. The beast still rises from the pit to oppose the will of God. Babylon – the epitome of worldly power, wealth and exploitation – still holds sway in the world's institutions. All of them are part of the world as it is, this strange amalgam of love and hate, beauty and cruelty, generosity and genocide, in which we are called to live the redeemed life.

Yet every image of horror in Revelation (and there are plenty of them!) is matched by a vision of the heavenly council chamber, the 'control centre' of history. Here the purpose of God is revealed: the 'scroll', in the visionary language, is opened. And here, seated on the throne of power and judgement, are two awesome figures. One is usually referred to simply as 'the One seated on the throne' – that's to say, the final Judge and Arbiter of everything. It is clear that he is 'the Lord God almighty'.

The other figure is described as a Lamb 'bearing the marks of slaughter'. That strange imagery – of innocence sacrificed, of suffering transformed – is equally clearly revealed as referring to Jesus, 'the Lamb of God who takes away the sin of the world'.

'Meekness and Majesty'

So here, on the throne of the universe sit two figures: meekness and majesty (to take words from Graham Kendrick's hymn) – benevolent power and suffering transformed. The world and its events are not out of control. There *is* a hand on the tiller of history, despite its apparent randomness and unpredictability. But the hand of power is not arbitrary or unfeeling. Far from it. For alongside the majesty is the meekness. The awesome figure on the throne is not alone. Beside him is the Lamb of God, bearing the marks of our pain, failure and sin.

The God of history is also the God of the incarnation. The one who comes to us in the dark with words of comfort is not unaware of what fear, pain and suffering entail. Our God is not a remote Cosmic Force, but *'Abba'*, the Father-God who in his Son has shared our pain.

As F W Faber's hymn *There's a Wideness in God's Mercy* puts it:
There is no place where earth's sorrows
are more felt than up in heaven;
there is no place where earth's failings
have such kindly judgement given.

This is the God who calms our fears.

QUESTIONS FOR GROUPS

BIBLE READING: Mark 6.45-52

1. Let's start on a positive note! Name two things that make you happy.

2. **Re-read Mark 6.50-51.** Looking back on your childhood, can you recall moments of fear? And what about your adult life? Does faith in God diminish fear, in your experience?

3. **Read John 10.10.** In her Closing Reflection for Session 3, Lucy Winkett speaks of life that is 'vibrant, imaginative, full of hope and grounded in love'. 'I saw God in his/her life' is a typical testimony. Describe someone in whom you have 'glimpsed' God?

4. **Read Matthew 6.34**. Worrying afflicts most of us (unlike Shirley Williams). Do you find Stephen Cottrell's practice of 'living in the moment' helpful [tracks 49 & 50]? Did Jesus mean that we shouldn't plan or provide for the future? What part does prayer play in this?

5. **Read Mark 6.48-50 and the box below.** What do you make of Pastor Wurmbrand's arithmetic and the conclusion he draws from it?

6. **Read 1 Peter 5.7 and the section 'Meekness and Majesty' on p 23.** A worried member of your church asks just how they might 'cast all their cares upon him'. How would you answer? Have you experienced 'the peace of God which passes all understanding' for which we pray regularly in church in the final Blessing?

7. **Read Matthew 17.20.** A mustard seed is tiny. But it has great potential for growth. Do you think your faith is still growing? Was there a time in your life when it grew quickly – or went into decline? Why?

8. What more could you or your church do to help your faith keep growing?

9. **Read John 11.25.** 'Pie in the sky when you die' is the old Marxist jibe at Christianity – don't worry about injustice, poverty, oppression, exploitation, it will all be all right in heaven. What does the Christian faith have to offer in *this* life?

10. '… events are not out of control. There *is* a hand on the tiller of history …' David Winter ends the course booklet by reminding us that God isn't remote and distant. He is *Abba*, Father – the Heavenly Father of the Lord's Prayer. What does that mean to you?

11. Stephen Cottrell's tribute to the Psalms as his favourite biblical book is very practical [track 56]. Share a favourite Bible passage that you turn to for comfort and strength when you are under pressure.

12. As this course comes to an end, you might want to plan ahead as a discussion group, a church or group of churches – depending on your answer to question 4!

Heard in a sermon: 'In a terrible Romanian prison, Pastor Wurmbrand counted the number of times "Fear not" appears in the Bible. On counting 366, he commented that this was typical of God's provision: One "don't be afraid" for every day – including a leap year!' (You might like to revisit track [58]. Whose arithmetic is right, we wonder? We haven't counted!)